Angular HTTP

Connecting to the REST API

Abdelfattah Ragab

Angular HTTP

Connecting to backend Rest APIs

Abdelfattah Ragab

Introduction

In this book, I explain everything you need to know about connecting to backend Rest APIs from your Angular application.
In this book, I will show you how to invoke different methods like GET, POST, and the like, how to use interceptors to inject an authentication token into every outgoing request, and much more.
We will cover all areas of calling Rest APIs with Angular.
By the end of this book, you will be able to call Rest APIs from your Angular application in any scenario.
Let us get started.

Understanding communication via HTTP

Most front-end applications need to communicate with a server via the HTTP protocol to download or upload data and access other back-end services. Angular provides a client HTTP API for Angular applications, the `HttpClient` service class in `@angular/common/http`.

Providing `HttpClient`

Before you can use the HttpClient in your application, you must configure it.
The `HttpClient` is provided with the help function `provideHttpClient`, which most applications include in the application providers in **app.config.ts**.

```
export const appConfig:
ApplicationConfig = {
  providers: [
    provideHttpClient(),
  ]
};
```

`provideHttpClient` accepts a list of optional feature configurations, to enable or configure the behavior of different aspects of the client.

By default, the `HttpClient` uses the `XMLHttpRequest` API to make requests. The `withFetch` function switches the client to use the Fetch API instead.

fetch is a more modern API and is available in some environments where `XMLHttpRequest` is not supported. It has some limitations, e.g. no upload progress events are generated.

```
export const appConfig:
ApplicationConfig = {
  providers: [
    provideHttpClient(
      withFetch(),
    ),
  ]
};
```

`HttpClient` service

You can then add the `HttpClient` service as a dependency of your components, services or other classes.
It is strongly recommended to create a separate service for API calls instead of calling the backend API directly from a component.
Here are some key reasons for this approach:
Separation of Concerns: Creating a service allows you to separate the logic for retrieving data from the presentation logic in your components. This makes your

components cleaner and easier to maintain, as they focus solely on user interface presentation and user interaction, while the service handles data retrieval and processing.

Reusability: By encapsulating API calls in a service, you can easily reuse the same service in multiple components. This reduces code duplication and promotes the DRY (Don't Repeat Yourself) principle, making your application more modular.

Centralized Error Handling: A service can centralize error handling for API calls. Instead of handling errors in each component, you can implement a consistent error handling strategy within the service. This can include logging errors, displaying notifications or retrying requests.

Improved Testability: Services can easily be mocked or stubbed in unit tests, allowing you to test components in isolation without relying on actual API calls. This leads to faster and more reliable tests.

In the following example, a list of users is retrieved from a backend API.

First, we create a service called `UserService` that will handle all API interactions related to users.

```typescript
// user.service.ts
import { Injectable } from '@angular/core';
import { HttpClient } from '@angular/common/http';
import { Observable } from 'rxjs';
```

```typescript
import { User } from './user.model'; // Assume we have a User model defined

@Injectable({
  providedIn: 'root'
})
export class UserService {
  private apiUrl = 'https://api.example.com/users'; // Replace with your API URL

  constructor(private http: HttpClient) {}

  // Method to fetch users
  getUsers(): Observable<User[]> {
    return this.http.get<User[]>(this.apiUrl);
  }
}
```

Note the generic type argument, which specifies that the data returned by the server is of type `User[]`. This argument is optional, and if you omit it, the returned data will be of type `any`.

Normally we use the environment variables to store the server URL similar to this.

```typescript
private apiUrl = environment.baseUrl + 'users';
```

Next, we will use this service in a component to display the list of users.

```typescript
// user-list.component.ts
import { Component, OnInit } from
'@angular/core';

import { User } from './user.model';
import { UserService } from
'./user.service';

// Assume we have a User model defined

@Component({
  selector: 'app-user-list',
  template: `
    <h1>User List</h1>
    <ul>
      @for (user of users; track
user.id) {
        <li>{{ user.name }}</li>
      }
    </ul>
  `
})
export class UserListComponent
implements OnInit {
  users: User[] = [];

  constructor(private userService:
UserService) {}
```

```typescript
  ngOnInit(): void {

this.userService.getUsers().subscribe(
      (data) => {
        this.users = data;
      },
      (error) => {
        console.error('Error fetching
users:', error);
      }
    );
  }
}
```

Making HTTP requests

`HttpClient` has methods that correspond to the
various HTTP verbs used to make requests, both to load
data and to apply mutations to the server. Each method
returns an RxJS observable which, if subscribed to,
sends the request and then prints the results when the
server responds.
On the following pages I will give you examples of
different scenarios of http requests. In some examples I
will show you the code of the backend written on NestJS
to give you a full idea of how things work, for example
when uploading a file or multiple files.
Suppose you are working on a hotel booking application
for a brand that has a number of hotels to which the
administrator can add new hotels, rooms, facilities, etc.

Users will be able to explore hotels and rooms and make reservations.

GET

`HttpClient` has a get method to read data from the backend.
According to Angular's best practices, you should create a service to connect to the backend.
So here you should have created the HotelsService in the **hotels.service.ts** file, which contains the getAll method as follows

```
getAll() {
  return
this.http.get(environment.API_URL +
'/hotels/all');
}
```

The get method accepts two parameters, the first of which is mandatory, namely the URL, while the second is optional, namely options.
The options parameter is an object with many option configurations. The most commonly used options are headers, params and responseType.

For example, if your backend server is configured to only accept the json format, you need to add the options headers as follows:

```
getAll() {
```

```
    return
this.http.get(environment.API_URL +
'/hotels/all', {
    headers: {
      'Content-Type': 'application/json',
    },
  });
}
```

According to best practices, you should not retrieve unnecessary data. Therefore, you must use pagination and read the first page of the hotels by passing the parameters of take and skip as follows:

```
getAll(take: number, skip: number) {
  return
this.http.get(environment.API_URL +
'/hotels/all', {
    params: {
      take,
      skip,
    },
    headers: {
      'Content-Type':
'application/json',
    },
  });
}
```

This time we use params and send take and skip to the backend server.

If you want to find a specific hotel by its identifier, simply add the identifier to the URL as follows:

```
getHotel(id: number) {
  return
this.http.get(environment.API_URL +
'/hotels/' + id, {
    headers: { 'Content-Type':
'application/json' },
  });
}
```

Passing header options depends on the configuration of your backend server, you may or may not need to add them.

POST

`HttpClient` has a post method to load data to the backend.
The first parameter is the URL, the second is the payload you want to send to the server, and the last is the options.
Let's say you want to add a new hotel, so here is the addHotel method

```
addHotel(hotel: any) {
  return
this.http.post(environment.API_URL +
'/hotels', hotel, {
    headers: {
      'Content-Type':
'application/json',
```

```
    },
  });
}
```

The second parameter is the `hotel` object to be added, and the headers option depends on your server configuration.
It looks as follows:

```
hotel: {
  title: 'Sheraton Athens',
  brand: 'Sheraton',
  starRating: 5,
  staffLanguages: ['English', 'Greek'],
  ...
}
```

Upload Single File

Let's say we have a FilesService **files.service.ts** where we upload images to the server. I will design the upload method as follows:

```
upload(file: any) {
  const formData = new FormData();
  formData.append('file', file);
  return
this.http.post(environment.API_URL +
'/storage/upload', formData);
}
```

You receive the file parameter from the input file in the template when the change event is triggered and pass this file to the service method

```
e.target.files[0]
```

The backend NestJS controller will look like this

```
@Post('upload')
@UseInterceptors(FileInterceptor('file')
)
async uploadFile(@UploadedFile() file:
Express.Multer.File) {
  if (file) return
this.storageService.upload(file);
}
```

Now you have the file, you can save it or whatever you want to do with it.

Here in the `StorageService`, I save it in the Firebase store and send the download URL back to the Angular application

```
async upload(file: any) {
  const storage = getStorage();
  const storageRef = ref(storage,
'images/' + file.originalname);
  const metadata = {
    contentType: file.mimetype,
  };
  const snapshot = await
uploadBytesResumable(
    storageRef,
    file.buffer,
    metadata,
  );

  const downloadUrl = await
getDownloadURL(snapshot.ref);
```

```
  return {
    name: file.originalname,
    type: file.mimetype,
    downloadUrl,
  };
}
```

Upload Multiple Files

To upload multiple files
```
uploadFiles(files: any) {
  const formData = new FormData();
  Array.from(files).forEach((file: any)
=> {
    formData.append('files[]', file);
  });
  return this.http.post(
    environment.API_URL +
'/storage/upload-files',
    formData,
  );
}
```
You receive the files parameter from the input file in the template when the change event is triggered and pass these files to the service method
```
e.target.files
```

In the NestJS application, I save the images in Firebase, group the results in an array and send it back to the Angular application

```typescript
async uploadFiles(files:
Array<Express.Multer.File>) {
  const savedFilesArray = [];
  const storage = getStorage();

  for (const file of files) {
    const fullPath = uuidv4() + '/' +
uuidv4() + extname(file.originalname);
    const metadata = {
      contentType: file.mimetype,
    };
    const storageRef = ref(storage,
fullPath);
    const snapshot = await
uploadBytesResumable(
      storageRef,
      file.buffer,
      metadata,
    );
    const downloadUrl = await
getDownloadURL(snapshot.ref);
    const fileObj = {
      originalName: file.originalname,
      mimeType: file.mimetype,
      downloadUrl,
      fullPath,
      size: file.size,
    };

    const savedFile = await
this.fileService.saveFile(fileObj);
```

```
      savedFilesArray.push(savedFile);
  }

  return savedFilesArray;
}
```

PUT

`HttpClient` has a put method to update data on the
backend.
The put method accepts three parameters, the url, the
body, and the options.
Here is how to update the hotel

```
updateHotel(hotel: any) {
  return
this.http.put(environment.API_URL +
'/hotels/' + hotel.id, hotel, {
    headers: {
      'Content-Type':
'application/json',
    },
  });
}
```

The url contains the ID of the hotel to be updated.
The second parameter is the hotel object that contains
the updates to be sent to the backend.

DELETE

`HttpClient` has a delete method to delete a resource on the backend.
Let's say you want to delete a room

```
deleteRoom(id: number) {
  return
this.http.delete(environment.API_URL +
'/rooms/' + id, {
    headers: { 'Content-Type':
'application/json' },
  });
}
```

You simply enter the ID in the url. It is not necessary to say that the deletion should be performed by the backend.

Interceptors

Interceptors are generally functions that you can run for each request, and have wide-ranging capabilities to influence the content and overall flow of requests and responses. You can install multiple interceptors that form an interceptor chain, in which each interceptor processes the request or response before passing it on to the next interceptor in the chain.
You can use interceptors to add authentication headers to outgoing requests to a specific API or to retry failed requests with exponential backoff.

The most common scenario is the auth interceptor, where we redirect the user to the login page if they are not authenticated.
In the following example, I redirect to the login page if no authentication has occurred and issue a new token based on the refresh token and retry the last failed request.

```typescript
import { HttpErrorResponse,
HttpInterceptorFn } from
'@angular/common/http';
import { PLATFORM_ID, inject } from
'@angular/core';
import { Router } from
'@angular/router';
import { catchError, switchMap,
throwError } from 'rxjs';
import { ACCESS_TOKEN, REFRESH_TOKEN }
from '../data/constants';
import { isPlatformBrowser } from
'@angular/common';
import { RefreshTokenService } from
'../services/refresh-token.service';

export const authInterceptor:
HttpInterceptorFn = (req: any, next:
any) => {
  const platformId =
inject(PLATFORM_ID);
  if (isPlatformBrowser(platformId)) {
    const authToken =
localStorage.getItem(ACCESS_TOKEN);
```

```typescript
    const router = inject(Router);
    const refreshTokenService =
inject(RefreshTokenService);
    if (authToken) {
      const authReq = req.clone({
        headers:
req.headers.set('Authorization', 'Bearer
' + authToken),
      });
      console.log('interceptor - auth
headers: ', authReq.headers);
      return next(authReq).pipe(
        catchError((error:
HttpErrorResponse) => {
          if (error.status === 401) {
            if
(req.url.endsWith('/refresh')) {

router.navigateByUrl('/login');
            } else {
              const refreshToken =
localStorage.getItem(REFRESH_TOKEN);

              if (refreshToken) {
                return
refreshTokenService.refreshToken(refresh
Token).pipe(
                  switchMap((result:
any) => {
```

```javascript
localStorage.setItem(ACCESS_TOKEN,
result.accessToken);

                    const retriedReq =
req.clone({
                        headers:
req.headers.set(
                            'Authorization',
                            'Bearer ' +
result.accessToken
                        ),
                    });
                    return
next(retriedReq);
                  })
                );
              }
            }
          }
          return throwError(() =>
error);
        })
      );
    } else return next(req);
  } else {
    return next(req);
  }
};
```

Observables

All `HttpClient` methods return an observable. At least one subscriber is required for the observable to be executed.
On your home page for example, in the onInit method you need to call the getAll method from the hotelsService to display a list of hotels.

```typescript
ngOnInit(): void {
  this.hotelsService.getAll(10,
0).subscribe((response: any) => {
    this.hotels = response[0];
  });
}
```

Promises

If you prefer promises and async/await, you can use lastValueFrom as follows:

```typescript
async ngOnInit(): Promise<void> {
  const response: any = await
lastValueFrom(this.hotelsService.getAll(1
0, 0));
  this.hotels = response[0];
}
```

Handling request failure

A network error may occur or the backend may not be able to process the request, resulting in an error being returned.

You can receive the error as follows:

```typescript
ngOnInit(): void {
  this.hotelsService.getAll(10,
0).subscribe({
    next: (response: any) => {
      this.hotels = response[0];
    },
    error: (e: any) => {
      console.log(e);
    },
  });
}
```

For async/await you can handle it as follows:

```typescript
async ngOnInit(): Promise<void> {
  try {
    const response: any = await
lastValueFrom(
      this.hotelsService.getAll(10, 0),
    );
    this.hotels = response[0];
  } catch (error) {
    console.error('Error:', error);
  }
}
```

`forkJoin` multiple HTTP requests

`forkJoin` is a powerful operator from the RxJS library that is commonly used in Angular applications to handle multiple asynchronous operations, especially when processing multiple HTTP requests. Here is a detailed explanation of how it works and when it should be used. Here is an example how to load all hotel details

```
loadHotelDetails() {
  this.isLoading = true;
  forkJoin([

this.hotelsService.getHotel(this.hotelId
),

this.hotelsService.getHotelImages(this.h
otelId),

this.hotelsService.getAllFacilities(),

this.hotelsService.getRooms(this.hotelId
),
  ])
    .pipe(first())
    .subscribe({
      next: (results: any) => {
        this.isLoading = false;
        this.hotel = results[0];
        this.images = results[1];
```

```
        this.hotelFacilities =
results[2];
        this.rooms = results[3];
      },
      error: (e) => {
        this.isLoading = false;
      },
    });
}
```

Conclusion

Congratulations! You have completed the book "Angular HTTP: Connecting to the REST API". Now you are able to connect to REST APIs from your Angular applications. Remember that learning Angular is an ongoing process. Practice makes perfect — build your own projects, experiment with the features you learn, and delve into the extensive online resources.
Thank you for joining me in my exploration of Angular. I wish you the best of luck on your programming journey. Have fun programming and good luck with your applications!

Media Attributions

Modern annual report magazine page flyer a company
catalog
Image by starline on Freepik

Www concept illustration
Image by storyset on Freepik

Don't miss out!

Receive an email when Abdelfattah Ragab publishes a new book. It's free and without obligation.

Also by Abdelfattah Ragab

Shippo is a multi-carrier shipping solution designed to streamline the shipping process for businesses of all sizes.

By integrating shipping into your application, you can create better types of e-commerce applications.

You will learn how to create the labels, calculate shipping costs, and get the fastest, cheapest, and best rates.

By the end of the book, you will be able to enable shipping in your Angular application and handle all kinds of scenarios.

Stripe Integration in Angular

Stripe is a leading payment processing platform that enables businesses to accept online payments.
By integrating payment processing into your application, you can create all kinds of e-commerce applications.

You will learn how to create the checkout session, how to use webhooks events and finally how to go live.
By the end of the book, you will be able to process payments in your Angular application and handle all kinds of scenarios.

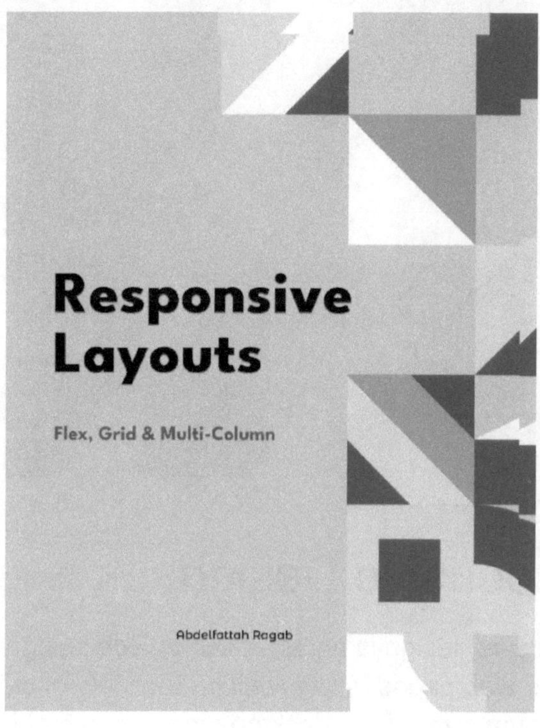

Responsive Design

Responsive design is an approach to web design that ensures web pages render well on a variety of devices and screen sizes, from desktop monitors to mobile phones. The primary goal of responsive design is to provide an optimal viewing experience, making it easy for users to read and navigate the site with minimal resizing, panning, and scrolling.

To learn more about responsive design, I advise you to read my book "**Responsive Layouts: Flex, Grid and Multi-Column**"
And read my book "**Responsive Design: All CSS responsive features**"

"**Angular Portfolio App Development**" will teach you how to create an online portfolio app that you can use to show off your skills to the world and your potential employers.

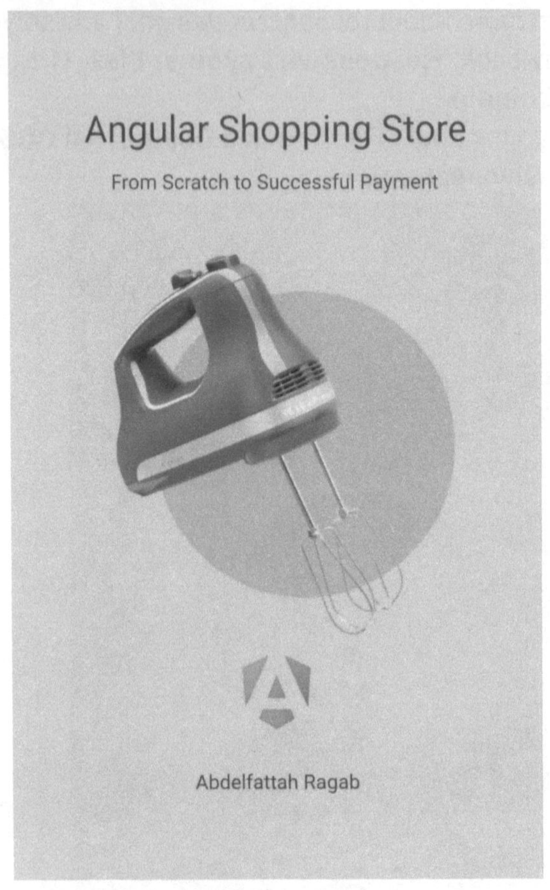

"**Angular Shopping Store**" a simple Angular e-commerce store.

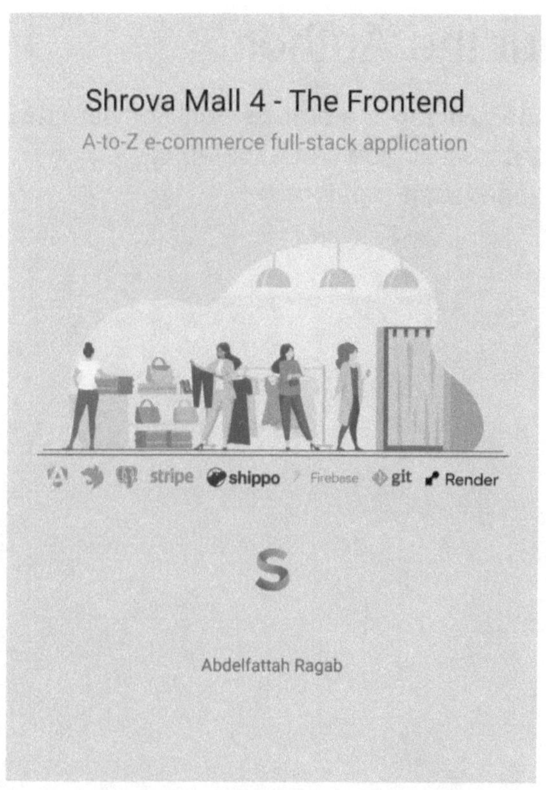

Once you are familiar with Angular, I recommend reading the book "**Shrova Mall**". This is a complete e-commerce solution that allows you to ship products to customers and accept payments online, among other things.

About the Author

Abdelfattah Ragab is a professional software developer with more than 20 years of experience. https://abdelfattah-ragab.com

About the Publisher

Abdelfattah Ragab is a highly qualified and experienced software developer with over 20 years of experience in the industry. Specializing in front-end development, Abdelfattah Ragab has a deep understanding of Angular, JavaScript, TypeScript, HTML and CSS. Read more at https://abdelfattah-ragab.com